Sports Illustrated KIDS

GAME-CHANGING COACHES

BASKETBALL'S BEST
COACHES

Influencers, Leaders, and Winners on the Court

written by Matt Chandler

CAPSTONE PRESS
a capstone imprint

T0011239

Published by Capstone Press, an imprint of Capstone
1710 Roe Crest Drive, North Mankato, Minnesota 56003
capstonepub.com

Copyright © 2024 by Capstone. All rights reserved. No part of this publication may be reproduced in whole or in part, or stored in a retrieval system, or transmitted in any form or by any means, electronic, mechanical, photocopying, recording, or otherwise, without written permission of the publisher.

SPORTS ILLUSTRATED KIDS is a trademark of ABG-SI LLC. Used with permission.

Library of Congress Cataloging-in-Publication Data
Names: Chandler, Matt, author.
Title: Basketball's best coaches : influencers, leaders, and winners on the court / by Matt Chandler.
Description: North Mankato, Minnesota : Capstone Press, [2024] | Series: Sports Illustrated Kids: game-changing coaches | Includes bibliographical references and index. | Audience: Ages 8-11 | Audience: Grades 4-6 | Summary: "Sometimes a basketball game's MVP is on the sidelines, not the court. Find out the facts about basketball's best coaches at both the professional and college level. Which coach has the best record? Who has won the most championships? And who has motived and led the most successful ball players? Turn these pages to find out!"— Provided by publisher.
Identifiers: LCCN 2023036488 (print) | LCCN 2023036489 (ebook) | ISBN 9781669063490 (hardcover) | ISBN 9781669063728 (paperback) | ISBN 9781669063537 (pdf) | ISBN 9781669063735 (epub) | ISBN 9781669063742 (kindle edition)
Subjects: LCSH: Basketball coaches—Juvenile literature. | Basketball—Coaching—Juvenile literature.
Classification: LCC GV885.3 .C43 2024 (print) | LCC GV885.3 (ebook) | DDC 796.32307/7—dc23/eng/20230805
LC record available at https://lccn.loc.gov/2023036488
LC ebook record available at https://lccn.loc.gov/2023036489

Editorial Credits
Editor: Mandy Robbins; Designer: Dina Her; Media Researcher: Jo Miller; Production Specialist: Tori Abraham

Image Credits
Alamy: ZUMA Press, Inc., 12, 23; Associated Press, 21, Eric Gay, 25, Mark Duncan, 17, Ron Schwane, 11, Steve Simoneau, 7, Tony Dejak, 10; Getty Images: ROBYN BECK, 19, GeorgePeters, design element (throughout); Icon Sportswire via AP Images, 27; Newscom: DAVID BERGMAN/KRT, 5; Shutterstock: Ekaterina_Mikhaylova, Cover, (top left), EV040, Cover, design element, Eyes wide, Cover, (bottom right), inspiring.team, Cover, design element, Lightspring, Cover, (bottom right), Luxury_Studio, design element (throughout), Oleksii Sidorov, Cover, (middle), Milano M, design element (throughout); Sports Illustrated: Andy Hayt, 15, Bill Frakes, 22, David E. Klutho, 9, Heinz Kluetmeier, 28, John Biever, 8, John W. McDonough, Cover, (top right), 13, Manny Millan, 14, 18, Simon Bruty, Cover, (bottom left)

All internet sites appearing in back matter were available and accurate when this book was sent to press.

Printed and bound in the USA. 5626

TABLE OF CONTENTS

INTRODUCTION
GREAT OR G.O.A.T.? 4

CHAPTER 1
CHAMPIONSHIP COACHES 6

CHAPTER 2
RECORD HOLDERS 16

CHAPTER 3
HALL OF FAMERS 20

CHAPTER 4
ALL-TIME WINNINGEST COACHES 24

Timeline 29
Glossary 30
Read More 31
Internet Sites 31
Index 32
About the Author 32

Words in **BOLD** are in the glossary.

GREAT OR G.O.A.T.?

There were two minutes left in the gold medal game at the 2000 Olympics. The United States led France by 10 points. Houston Rockets head coach Rudy Tomjanovich was leading Team USA. The United States was about to win the gold medal. Instead of beginning to celebrate, Tomjanovich called a time-out.

Although the game was almost over, Tomjanovich refused to relax. He coached to the final buzzer, barking instructions at some of the greatest players in the National Basketball Association (NBA). It worked. Tomjanovich led his team to the Olympic gold medal!

Tomjanovich won NBA championships in 1994 and 1995. He won more than 500 games in his Hall of Fame career. Yet today, his name is rarely mentioned among the greatest coaches of all time. Get ready to learn about the coaches who were so great, they could outshine a two-time NBA championship-winning coach.

Coach Rudy Tomjanovich
during the 2000 Olympics

CHAPTER 1

CHAMPIONSHIP COACHES

As a player for the New York Knicks, Phil Jackson won the NBA championship in 1970 and in 1973. After retiring as a player in 1980, Jackson went on to become a superstar coach. He led the Chicago Bulls to three straight NBA titles in 1991, 1992, and 1993.

Jackson led Michael Jordan, Scottie Pippen, Dennis Rodman, and the rest of the Bulls to another three-peat. They won the NBA championship in 1996, 1997, and 1998!

Critics wondered if Jackson was a great coach or if he just had the perfect team of players in Chicago. He proved his critics wrong. Jackson left Chicago and went to Los Angeles. There he coached the Lakers to titles in 2000, 2001, and 2002. He did it again in 2009 and 2010!

Phil Jackson and Michael Jordan during a 1996 game

Fact

Jackson was so smart that the New Jersey Nets named him assistant coach while he was still playing in 1978.

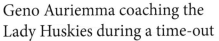
Geno Auriemma coaching the Lady Huskies during a time-out

Geno Auriemma has coached the University of Connecticut (UConn) Lady Huskies since 1985. Auriemma has won a record 11 National Collegiate Athletic Association (NCAA) championships as head coach of the Lady Huskies.

Auriemma's approach to the game is one reason players love to play for him. He makes working hard fun through honesty, trust, and working toward a common goal. That approach has led him to develop some of the biggest stars in the Women's National Basketball Association (WNBA). Superstars Sue Bird, Diana Taurasi, Maya Moore, Tina Charles, and Breanna Stewart all played for Auriemma at UConn.

Geno Auriemma cuts down the net after leading the Lady Huskies to the 2014 NCAA Women's National Championship.

"I just want the players to understand that the one constant in our program is that we want to make sure we play hard and have fun."—Geno Auriemma

Jerry Sloan was a head coach in the NBA for almost 30 years, but he was never able to win an NBA championship. On the opposite end, there is a small group of coaches who won NBA titles in their **rookie** season as head coaches!

Coach Tyronn Lue during a 2016 Cavaliers game

Tyronn Lue gives LeBron James a tip during a 2016 Cavaliers game.

Tyronn Lue was named head coach of the Cleveland Cavaliers partway through the 2015–16 season. Under his leadership, the Cavs won the Eastern Conference and made it to the NBA Finals.

The Golden State Warriors took a 3–1 lead against the Cavs in that series. They were one win away from the championship, but Lue never gave up. His team came back for three straight wins and the first NBA title in the history of the Cavaliers!

Fact

The latest rookie coach to win an NBA championship was Nick Nurse. He led the Toronto Raptors to the top in 2019.

Steve Kerr won five NBA championships as a player. But few successful players go on to become successful coaches.

Kerr was hired as the head coach of the Golden State Warriors in 2014. Kerr had never coached in the NBA. He didn't let that stop him. Kerr led his team to the best record in the NBA at 67–15. He coached superstars Steph Curry, Draymond Green, and Klay Thompson to the playoffs. Kerr led the Warriors to the NBA title as a rookie head coach.

He didn't let up. In his first eight seasons as a head coach, Kerr led his team to the finals six times. He's won four NBA titles with the Warriors.

Coach Steve Kerr and Steph Curry during a 2019 Golden State Warriors game.

"I've been blessed with an amazing group of guys in my first year. I can't believe how lucky I am." —Steve Kerr

Los Angeles Lakers center Bob McAdoo floated a soft jumper as time ran out. The Lakers beat the Philadelphia 76ers 114–104 to win the 1982 NBA championship! Fans flooded the court as players and coaches celebrated the title. Among them was Lakers head coach, Pat Riley. It was his first year as an NBA head coach!

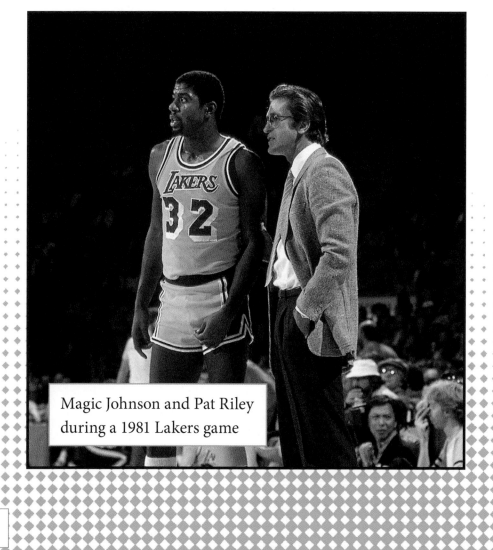

Magic Johnson and Pat Riley during a 1981 Lakers game

Riley led future Hall of Fame players Kareem Abdul-Jabbar, Magic Johnson, and McAdoo to a title. He used a new style of play called "Showtime" offense. The players loved this fast-paced, dynamic way of play. Riley won three more NBA titles with the Lakers and one with the Miami Heat. Riley retired from coaching in 2008.

Laker Legend

Pat Riley's role with the Lakers was much more than his nine seasons as the team's head coach. Riley began his Lakers career as a bench player for the team in 1970. He played five full seasons in Los Angeles, winning the NBA championship in 1972. Once he retired, Riley became a commentator for Lakers television broadcasts. He moved on to be an assistant coach, helping the Lakers win the 1980 NBA title. Over a 20-year span, Riley won titles with the Lakers as a player, assistant coach, and head coach!

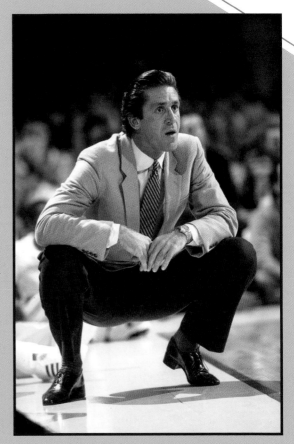

CHAPTER 2

RECORD HOLDERS

Pat Summitt was just 22 years old when she was named head coach of the University of Tennessee Lady Volunteers in 1974. She led the Lady Vols for the next 38 seasons!

When Summitt began her career, the NCAA tournament was for men's teams only. It wasn't until the 1980s that women were allowed to play in the college postseason. Once the door was open, Summitt led her team to the NCAA tournament 31 times. That was a new NCAA record.

Summitt's teams won eight national championships over three decades. Her success led Summitt to receive multiple offers to coach the men's team at Tennessee. She turned them all down.

"I want to keep doing the right things for women all the time."—Pat Summitt

The Summitt of Coaching

In her final year at Tennessee, Summitt earned nearly $2 million, but she fought for nearly 40 years to get there. As a rookie coach, Summitt was paid $250 per month to coach the Lady Vols. She also had to take the uniforms home and wash them after games and drive the team bus!

Pat Summitt celebrates leading the Lady Vols to the 2007 NCAA women's championship.

Larry Brown (right) and Danny Manning during a 1988 Jayhawks game

More than 22,000 fans cheered as the clock ran down in Game Five of the 2004 NBA Finals. The Detroit Pistons defeated the Los Angeles Lakers 100–87 to win the NBA title. Pistons head coach Larry Brown had led his team to a huge **upset** over the Lakers.

The win gave Brown a new coaching record. Brown had led the Kansas Jayhawks to the NCAA championship in 1988. Now he was the only coach in the history of basketball to lead a team to an NCAA championship and an NBA title.

Brown also holds another NBA record. He is the only head coach to lead eight different teams to the playoffs. Brown won playoff games as head coach of the Nuggets, Nets, Spurs, Clippers, Pacers, 76ers, Pistons, and Hornets.

Larry Brown celebrating with the Pistons after winning the 2004 NBA championship

CHAPTER 3
HALL OF FAMERS

Most NBA coaches roam the sidelines in a suit and tie. In 1966, the head coach of the Boston Celtics wore a uniform. Celtics legend Bill Russell served as a **player-coach** for three seasons. It was the 1966–67 season that was historic. Celtics coach Red Auerbach stepped down in 1966. He tapped Russell to become the team's new leader. Russell broke the color barrier. He became the first Black coach in league history.

Russell didn't like people suggesting he got the job because of his skin color. At the time he said:

"I was offered it because Red figured I could do it."—Bill Russell

Russell proved Auerbach was right. He won two NBA titles as a player-coach.

Fact

Russell fought for equality his entire life. In 1961, when playing for the Celtics, two teammates were refused service in a restaurant before a Celtics game. He and several other players boycotted the game.

Tara VanDerveer coaching Stanford during the 2012 Final Four

In December 2020, Stanford women's head coach Tara VanDerveer led her team to victory over Pacific University 104–61. The win was VanDerveer's 1,099th as a head coach. It made VanDerveer the winningest women's basketball coach in history, breaking Pat Summitt's record. She led her team to 14 Final Four appearances, won three NCAA titles, and was elected to the Hall of Fame.

In the first 26 drafts for the WNBA, Stanford had 28 players chosen. Those players credit VanDerveer for helping them develop into professional athletes.

VanDerveer and her players during a 2011 game

CHAPTER 4
ALL-TIME WINNINGEST COACHES

If you measure the greatest coach by wins, San Antonio Spurs coach Gregg Popovich is the G.O.A.T. "Pop," as he is known, has racked up over 1,350 wins—more than any coach in NBA history.

Pop broke the record on March 11, 2022. The Spurs were hosting the Utah Jazz. Pop led his team to a hard-fought 104–102 win. It was his 1,336th regular season win. Like many of the greatest coaches, he wanted to share the honor with his players.

"All of us share in this record. It's not mine. It's ours."—Gregg Popovich

Pop has won five NBA championships and has been named NBA Coach of the Year three times!

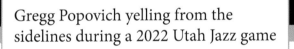

Gregg Popovich yelling from the sidelines during a 2022 Utah Jazz game

Steve Kerr was **mentored** by Popovich early in his career. Kerr called Pop "an amazing coach and an amazing man."

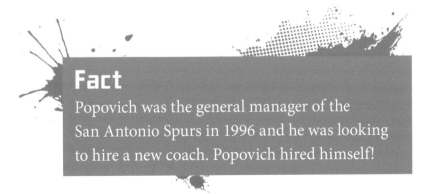

Fact

Popovich was the general manager of the San Antonio Spurs in 1996 and he was looking to hire a new coach. Popovich hired himself!

With more than 71,000 fans cheering, Duke Blue Devils Coach Mike Krzyzewski walked toward center court smiling. Streamers fell from the ceiling as coaches and players offered hugs. Coach K had just led the Blue Devils to the 2015 NCAA championship!

It was Coach K's fifth national title. He retired from Duke University after 42 seasons. His 1,202 wins are tops in the regular season. He has also won 101 NCAA tournament games in his career—more than any other coach. Coach K is known for having 68 players drafted into the NBA!

"He's not afraid to tell you the truth. And he's willing to hear you out."—Jason Kidd, Dallas Mavericks coach, speaking of Coach K.

Fact

Coach K is the only basketball coach to ever lead a team to three Olympic gold medals in a row.

Mike Krzyzewski celebrating with the Blue Devils after winning the 2015 NCAA championship

THE GREATEST

The players are the most important part of a basketball team. But behind every great team of players, is usually a superstar coach guiding them to greatness!

It can be fun to **debate** who the greatest coaches in basketball history are. Does a coach have to coach for a long time to be the best? Do they have to win lots of championships? The greatest means different things for every fan. Who would you choose out of the coaches in this book? Do you think other coaches should have been included?

Pat Riley coaching the Lakers in the 1983 NBA Finals

TIMELINE

1966 The Boston Celtics' Bill Russell becomes the first Black head coach in league history.

1981 The Lakers hire Pat Riley as a first-time head coach midway through the season. He leads the team to the NBA championship.

1996 The San Antonio Spurs name Gregg Popovich head coach. "Pop" would go on to lead the Spurs to five NBA titles and become the winningest coach in NBA history.

2008 Pat Summitt leads the Lady Vols to the national championship. It becomes the third decade Summitt has won a national title at Tennessee.

2010 Larry Brown sets the record for most teams coached in the playoffs. The Charlotte Hornets become the eighth team Brown took to the postseason.

2015 As a rookie head coach, Steve Kerr leads the Golden State Warriors to the best record in the NBA. He also wins his first NBA championship as a coach.

2016 Duke Coach Mike Krzyzewski becomes the first coach in history to lead a team to three straight Olympic gold medals.

2020 Stanford coach Tara VanDerveer becomes the winningest women's coach in history with her 1,099th career victory.

GLOSSARY

CRITIC (KRIT-ik)—a person who tells the good and bad of something

DEBATE (di-BAYT)—a discussion in which people offer different opinions

MENTOR (MEN-tur)—a wise and faithful adviser or teacher

PLAYER-COACH (PLAY-ur-COCHE)—when a player on the team also acts as the coach

ROOKIE (RUH-kee)—someone in their first year of doing something

UPSET (UHP-set)—a win by a team that was expected to lose

READ MORE

Berglund, Bruce. *Basketball GOATs*. North Mankato, MN: Capstone Press, 2022.

Chandler, Matt. *Basketball Biographies for Kids: The Greatest NBA and WNBA Players from the 1960s to Today*. Berkeley, CA: Rockridge Press, 2022.

Monnig, Alex. *Basketball*. Edina, MN: A & D Xtreme, 2022.

INTERNET SITES

Basketball Hall of Fame
hoophall.com/

Junior NBA
jr.nba.com/

Sports Illustrated Kids: Basketball
sikids.com/basketball

INDEX

Auerbach, Red, 20
Auriemma, Geno, 8–9

Brown, Larry, 18–19, 29

Hall of Fame, 4, 15, 23

Jackson, Phil, 6, 7

Kerr, Steve, 12, 13, 25, 29
Krzyzewski, Mike, 26, 27, 29

Lue, Tyronn, 10, 11

Nurse, Nick, 11

Olympics, 4, 5, 26, 29

Popovich, Gregg, 24–25, 29

records, 8, 12, 16, 18, 19, 23, 24, 26, 29
Riley, Pat, 14–15, 28, 29
Russell, Bill, 20, 21, 29

Sloan, Jerry, 10
Summitt, Pat, 16, 17, 23, 29

Tomjanovich, Rudy, 4, 5

VanDerveer, Tara, 22, 23, 29

ABOUT THE AUTHOR

Matt Chandler is the author of more than 85 children's books, including *Side-by-Side Baseball Stars*, the 2015 Outstanding Children's Book Award winner from the American Society of Journalists and Authors. Matt lives in New York with his wife Amber, children, Zoey and Ollie, and his four-legged friends, Lola and George. Learn more at www.mattchandlerwriting.com